MIDSOMER NORTON AND RADSTOCK

IN OLD PHOTOGRAPHS

MIDSOMER NORTON
AND
RADSTOCK
IN OLD PHOTOGRAPHS

COLLECTED BY
CHRIS HOWELL

ALAN SUTTON
1988

Alan Sutton Publishing Limited
Brunswick Road · Gloucester

First published 1988

British Library Cataloguing in Publication Data

Midsomer Norton and Radstock in old photographs.
1. Avon. Midsomer Norton, history.
Radstock, history
I. Howell, Chris
942.3'97

ISBN 0 86299 552 3

4 7 104566 120164

Typesetting and origination by
Alan Sutton Publishing Limited.
Printed in Great Britain by
WBC Print Limited.

CONTENTS

AN AERIAL PHOTOGRAPH OF MIDSOMER NORTON as it was in 1946. The road running from top to bottom is the one from Paulton to Chilcompton.

INTRODUCTION

This book is not like any of the others that I have compiled about the area – but, then again, it's not meant to be. The publisher, Alan Sutton Publishing, is putting together a series that covers the whole of the country and, in order to comply with his plans, the book includes more pictures and less text than the others. To begin with I was unsure that such a format was to my liking, but then I thought of all the unused photographs of the district that may not otherwise ever have been published. A few of these may not be of the highest quality, but I have always felt that when there is only one copy of a picture available it should be used whatever its condition. So, the book has given me the opportunity to print a great number of pictures that would, in all probability, have remained in boxes.

Then there is a great amount of unused material that I still have on tape. A number of the people whom I have quoted were born more than a hundred years ago, and what they had to say must have some importance in the context of local history. (As a matter of interest, I have worked out that the average age of these people is greater than the average age of the pictures!)

Perhaps the single thing that made me want to work on the book was when I was told that – entirely without my knowledge – I had printed a picture of my paternal grandfather (who was born in 1855!) and grandmother in a book that I had written on Somerset. It was a very strange feeling – indeed, weird – to find them there in that fashion. Until that time I had not really appreciated what it had meant to others who had found their family or memories in similar books. Perhaps one of the faded pictures in this one might just do the same for someone else.

Finally, the book has given me the opportunity to print a few more stories and pictures of Charlie Fry, whom once I intended to have a book of his own. Charlie was a man who aroused enormous goodwill in all who knew him. He was 15 at the turn of the century. Unwillingly he became involved in the bloodiest of wars and returned mentally and physically scarred. But, for all of his eccentricity and peculiar ways, he was a gentleman.

I was born in the row of houses at the bottom of Charlie Fry's fields. I did not know him as well as Alan Chivers did – and I regret that – but his was probably the first voice I heard from outside my home – Leslie Shearn says that when Charlie called his cows, every one within a three-mile radius turned up! It was almost certainly one particular photograph of Charlie that caused me to write my first book, so this one is dedicated – for Alan Chivers – to Charlie.

Chris Howell
Chilcompton
June 1988

A LOCAL FARMER WITH HIS FAMILY, pictured in 1898.

Midsomer Norton

A DISCUSSION GROUP meets beneath the Jubilee lamp in the late 1920s. 'Diff'rent now, innit? Old Charlie Mattick's shop on the right, where I used to go in an' watch him mending harness. Lawyer Thatcher's office. Stocks, the butcher. Wills, the tailor. And that lovely lamp.' (RJ.)

A GENERAL VIEW OF THE TOWN seen from the Somerset and Dorset railway line in 1910.

'THASS WHERE I WERE BROUGHT UP, just to the right of where they'm standin'. Where that chap's standin' at the back's where Lucky Purnell used tuh live – he were a butcher an' I used tuh go in there to buy me mother's pork chops. Course thass all pulled down now.' (RJ.)

CLAPTON ROAD in the 1930s soon after the houses were built.

CLEVEDON ROAD as it was at the beginning of the 1920s.

THE STEVENS' FARM at the bottom of Millard's Hill in Welton before the Great War.

THIS PICTURE OFTEN SEEMS TO PUZZLE PEOPLE, probably because there are now shops on either side of the High Street at this point. It was taken looking up towards Stones Cross in 1912. Shearns, the butchers and Speeds, the builders, were on the right beyond the lady in the apron.

ONE OF THE EARLIEST PICTURES OF STONES CROSS that I have seen. It was probably taken in the 1890s, before the signpost was attached to the street lamp.

WOOLF'S STONES CROSS COMMERCIAL HOTEL was advertising both garaging for motor cars and traps for hire when this was taken in 1911. Notice the wooden pushchair!

'THIS IS MORE LIKE IT! Hundreds of times we've walked across those flashes – dared one another to do it before we went to school. Thass Beale's paper shop on the left.' (RJ.) This must have been taken in around 1904 – the children are far more interested in the camera than in the tree straining at its hawser in the background.

'OUTSIDE THE PALLADIUM. There's a man cleanin' the path outside Mr Simpkins's house – one of the mining instructors at Norton Hill Colliery at the time. Must have bin taken about 1900 or so.' (RJ.)

EVEN IN 1935, when this was taken, there was very little traffic in the High Street. To the left of the cyclist is a sign for the Ashton Gate off-licence and, to the right, another for the Three Horseshoes pub.

A SLIGHTLY LATER VIEW OF THE RIVER than the one opposite but still the river flows quite quickly over the 'flashes'. When the sluice traps were opened the force of the water cleaned any debris or deposits off the bed of the river.

THE CONSERVATORY on the east end of The Hollies (in 1897) was first replaced by the town's library which in turn went to make way for the present council offices.

THIS WAS PROBABLY TAKEN ON A SATURDAY C. 1912. Behind the three fellows – turned out in their best bib and tucker – can be seen the ladder of workmen packing up at Welch's shop and, coming out from the Island, is a laden horse-drawn brake, probably taking a football team off for the afternoon.

ANOTHER QUIET MOMENT (in 1908) and everything stops for the photographer – even the horse and the man cleaning the drinking fountain.

WORK UNDERWAY ON THE ROAD VERGES outside the Wesleyan School c. 1910.

'DEAR ELS,' it says on the back of this postcard. 'This is where I went Wed it is a pretty place do you know any one on here with love from Will.' Will, who I presume is the lad in the foreground, posted the card in 1913.

MIDSOMER NORTON'S ALMSHOUSES as they were in 1909 – they were then fourteen years old, a couple of years older than the girl on the left who is standing at the gate of what had been the first bank in the town in the 1860s. Notice that the river was open much further at that time.

TO THE LEFT OF THE TOWN HALL is a later bank – the Wilts and Dorset – now Lloyds. Cast into the base of the Jubilee Lamp is 'Victoria 1897'.

A QUIET MOMENT BY THE RIVER in 1908. Mr Beale, with time to spare, can just be seen standing outside his shop in the centre of the picture.

'LOOK AT THE HAT THAT YOUNGSTER'S GOT ON! On the left there was Mr Lusensky's shop – a Russian, nice chap, all right. My brothers worked for him – learnt the way to cut hair and shave.' (RJ.)

A SIMILAR PICTURE TAKEN THE SAME YEAR — 1906. Although it was an original 'Chapman' postcard, identical copies were available as published by Purnell & Sons, Paulton, Radstock & Midsomer Norton!

THIS WAS TAKEN IN AROUND 1910, before the river was permanently diverted to its present course and the culvert through the Mill sealed off. The newly-built Masonic Hall is in the centre. 'I can remember them puttin' that place there. Used to watch the men in their white coats chippin' away with mallets an' chisels. Stone carvers, see.' (RJ.)

THE MEADOW, once the home of Midsomer Norton's gymkhanas and flower shows, was originally part of the park belonging to Norton House (where Park Way now stands). It is now the site of Somervale School.

NORTON HOUSE IN WINTERTIME. I have a sale catalogue from 1908 when it changed hands. Among the 1035 items listed were a thermal bath (with gas fittings), an ice-cream machine and an 'X-Ray Outfit, complete, including 6in. Induction Coil (by Wendham), with Crooks, Tube and Screen, Battery, &c.'.

DR ALEXANDER WAUGH'S HOUSE at the bottom of Silver Street. This is where the Doctor's grandson, Evelyn Waugh, spent his holidays as a schoolboy and to which he returned when it was sold in 1953. 'The house had failed to sell at £3,000. Paid a final visit to the house without emotion.'

SILVER STREET in around 1905. Evelyn Waugh's father, Arthur, who lived at the bottom on the right, called it 'The Avenue' in his book, *One Man's Road* – 'Our favourite walk led us up the hill, under a stately avenue of trees'.

Radstock

A GENERAL VIEW ACROSS RADSTOCK towards Frome Hill in 1929.

'NOW, THOSE TERRACES ARE THE ONES IN WELTON HOLLOW, going down to Five Arches and behind the big tree in the middle was what they called Rifle Terrace – two ranks going down the sloping field so close together you could shake hands across the alleyway. This is before Somervale Road was built – say 1908 or 9.' (CL.)

'WHITELANDS TERRACE – up at Tyning. Most of what used to be there's gone now. They were built for to house miners – an' all on'em had pigs!' (CL.)

A QUIET MOMENT IN COOMBEND in 1904.

WASHDAY ON FROME HILL in around 1903, just one year after the new Methodist Church had been opened by the Mayor of Swindon.

ANOTHER VIEW OF FROME HILL with, in the foreground, the timber yard of W.J. Taylor whose main premises were at Steam Mills, in Midsomer Norton. This yard was managed by his son Ernest and timber was delivered to the site by traction engines towing four wheeled wagons with wooden block brakes.

'NO, THAT'S NOT A BEER BARREL — could be tar. They used to deliver beer proper in they days — barrels an' two gallon jars. An' if you went to draw some off Father'd say, "Keep whistlin' while you're drawin' it, won't you!".' (CL.)

'NO-ONE WAS IN A BIG HURRY, were they? This must've bin about 1900 – quite a while before they put the new Somervale Road through on the left. That tree is hangin' over from the rectory gardens and just over the wall the parson used to have a dip place – where he could go to have a cold bath in the open air.' (CL.)

THIS WAS TAKEN IN AROUND 1895. 'And that's my grandmother in the big cape. Grandfather was a foreman on the road but he died early leaving her with seven children and she kept them by taking in washing. They lived in an old cottage at the top of Church Hill – made of rubble and mud. One day the whole corner of the building just fell away.' (GB.)

GEORGE COOMBS (with the beard) and fellow directors of his brewing and hotel company at the turn of the century, perhaps in 1900 when it was agreed 'to reduce the principal gravities by 1lb. per barrel to meet the increase in duty (to finance the Boer War). The Directors also decided to discontinue their trade in ale @ 6d. per gall, raising the price to 7d. per gall, except in special cases when special terms were to be made to those farmers who still desire to purchase a men's ale @ 6d.'.

'GALLONS AND GALLONS AND GALLONS OF BEER came out of that place – it used to be brought out from the back of the market on two-wheeled floats.' (CL.) Nevertheless, in 1901 the company wrote to the Oakhill Brewery firm asking for 'more favourable terms in view of the low terms and prices afforded to the general public by the Oakhill Brewery Company themselves'.

'SEE THE FARMWORKER ON THE LEFT THERE? With yorks round his trousers? Nobody were in a hurry in they days – all on 'em lookin' at the photographer, see. Or at the dog.' (CL.)

'BLIMEY, STILL BIKES AND CARTS. Still not a car in sight! I wish t'were like it now!' (CL.) 'I remember when the first car came through the village. It had wooden wheels like they had on carriages. A hell of a height and no windscreen. Tiller steering, not a wheel. I was at school and t'was playtime and a chap saw it heading our way and cycled two miles to tell us. The schoolmaster let us stay out a bit longer and we all lined up along the fence. We were thunderstruck!' (JG.)

'RADSTOCK MARKET? Buy anything. There were butchers stalls, fish stalls, sweet stalls, bread stalls, vegetable stalls. And there was a cheese stall chock-a-block with such cheese. Sixpence a pound and if you could tell the man which was which he'd cut off a big piece and give you a taste.' (EB.)

THE WESLEYAN CHURCH in Fortescue Road in around 1907. The shops on the right were built some ten years earlier.

WELLS HILL in the 1920s. The ladies on the right are viewing the latest pictures in the window of Mr White's photography shop.

THIS POSTCARD WAS SENT TO BARTON, near Morton-in-Marsh in 1904. 'Spending weekend here and it's lovely after the rain', which no doubt helped to fill Snail's Brook in the foreground.

SOUTH HILL HOUSE, in Radstock, home of George McMurtrie the mine manager. 'And there's his geraniums what the miners threatened to hit down for him during the 1926 strike.' (CL.)

'THAT USED TO FLOOD THREE OR FOUR TIMES A YEAR DOWN THERE BY THE MILL. Half-way up the cottage doors opposite. Folk in 'em used to belt upstairs and out the back where the ground was higher. Used to be a chap called Grist live there, put up with it for years before he moved.' (CL.) Grist from the mill?

GEORGE COOMBS AND HIS WIFE FRANCES in the grounds of Radstock House in 1900.

RADSTOCK'S VICTORIA HALL AND CENOTAPH in the early 1920s.

SECTION THREE

Coalmining

MIDDLE PIT in Radstock in October 1905, soon after modernisation work had taken place. The wording on the coal trucks reads: 'The Earl Waldegrave – Radstock Collieries'.

LUDLOWS PIT in the 1920s, sometime after the steel headgear had been erected to replace an earlier wooden one. Middle Pit can be seen in the background.

REG JAMES AND WORKMEN on the Duke of Somerset's estate load the Sentinel steam wagon with timber for pit props in the Radstock collieries, soon after the Great War.

UPPER WRITHLINGTON COLLIERY. The pit was operational from 1805 until 1898 but the buildings beyond the chimney were retained as offices and as the home of the mine manager.

'I RECKON THIS WAS THE 1912 STRIKE – could have been the 1905 one but I was too young to remember that one. Radstock had a bad reputation in those days and miners were considered such a rough lot – there'd always be fights after the market on Saturdays – round on Blood Ground. This lot were there to keep law and order. The constables were billetted at the Victoria Hall – sleeping on matresses, and the sergeants were put into private homes – my uncle and aunt had one.' (GB.)

AN UNKNOWN MINER wearing the infamous guss and crook. 'I wore one o' they fer seven years. Terrible, my son, the blood did come out yer skin and you did treat yourself wie yer own urine from the piss pot. But once yer skin did get hard that were a very useful tool to have and you couldn't do owt wie'out the guss. If half a ton o' coal come off the rails I could lift'n back on wie the guss. I could.' (BC.)

SPRINGFIELD PIT (in the foreground) and Old Mills Pit soon after the turn of the century. The formation of the well-known slag heap has already begun and can be seen to the right of the picture.

MINERS ABOUT TO DESCEND THE SHAFT in one of the Radstock collieries in the 1920s. 'They're going down on top of the cage – checking that the guides are running freely. Used to do that twice a day.' (RJ.)

MIDSOMER NORTON seen through the overhead tramway that was built in around 1910 ('I can mind when he were put up' – (RJ)) to carry slag from Norton Hill pit to the waste tip in the Rackvernal field.

LOUIS BEAUCHAMP – the co-owner of the pit with his brother Frank – surveys the scene from the gantry that was built by Norton Harty, engineers from Tipton in Staffordshire.

NORTON HILL PIT in around 1910. The chap on the right is sorting out waste that was dumped before the bridge in the background was finished — 'wallin' it not fer it to fall down on the railway line'. (RJ.)

'THESE THINGS WEREN'T HEARD OF UNTIL 1910 or thereabouts. Until then if you came up injured they threw you in the back of a coal cart and that's how you had to go home.' (GB.)

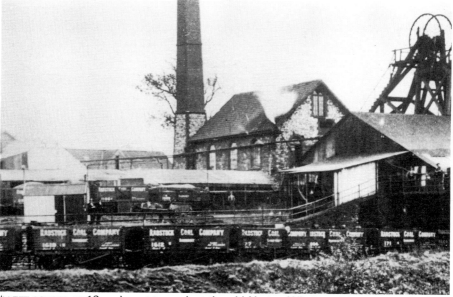

'I LEFT SCHOOL AT 13 and went to work at the old Norton Hill pit pushing empty tubs for a shillin' a day. Six bob a week wie druppence off for the union. Five an' ninepence to take home to get the black off of me.' (ST.)

THE SCENE AT NORTON HILL COLLIERY on 10 April, 1908, some ten or twelve hours after the devastating explosion that killed ten men underground with a blast that shook the whole of Midsomer Norton. A number of pit ponies were also killed – 'Mr Haydon, the Vet, had to go down to puncture them to let the gasses out so's they could be brought up and be buried in a quarry near the pit'. (IC.)

THE FUNERAL OF ONE OF THE NORTON HILL DISASTER VICTIMS in Radstock. Leading the mourners is Frank Beauchamp, the owner of the colliery. Behind the man with the flowers is the manager, Robert Bennett, who spent the three days following the explosion working underground. To the left and behind Bob Bennett is Herbert Attwood, the under-manager, who was in the first party to enter the pit after the blast.

POLICE MAKING THEIR WAY TO THE CEMETERY IN MIDSOMER NORTON during another of the funerals that followed the tragedy at Norton Hill.

MINERS WITH THEIR WIVES AND CHILDREN crowd the approaches as another coffin is borne from the funeral service to the cemetery in Church Lane.

SECTION FOUR

Royal Visit

ON 23 JUNE, 1909, the Prince and Princess of Wales came to Midsomer Norton to present specially minted medals to those involved in the rescue work following the pit disaster at Norton Hill the previous year.

THIS POSTCARD was a special commemorative one made up by the local photographer F.G. Steggles and features not only the rescue party but also a number of other local celebrities. 'Richard Batt, gentleman farmer; W.J. Taylor of the sawmills; George Delve, my schoolmaster; Ethelbert Horne from Downside; Caleb Stock, the butcher, gosh, there are so many stories to be told there.' (LS.)

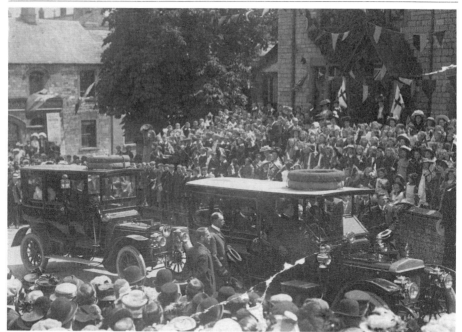

THE ROYAL CONVOY was a few minutes late when it arrived in Radstock from Longleat where the party here stayed overnight. Nonetheless the cars stopped long enough for the children to sing 'God Save the Prince of Wales'.

THE ROYAL COUPLE are actually leaving Midsomer Norton here (on their way to Wells for a service to mark 1000 years of the Bishopric there). The vehicles pause (again!) at the Wesleyan School for the assembled schoolchildren to sing.

THE PRINCE OF WALES addressing the invited guests at the presentation ceremony. 'I was taken up there with a nurse to see it all. I remember a narrow path between woods, crowds and crowds of people and Norton House on the left. But when you're four years old some things don't mean a lot, do they?' (LS.)

CROWDS WAIT AT THE BOTTOM OF SILVER STREET for a glimpse of the Prince and Princess once they leave Norton House.

MORE WOULD-BE SIGHTSEERS. One lad seems to be studying form while a group of older fellows appear to be off to the White Hart for a swift pint.

'THAT'S WHERE WE SANG FROM — that was my classroom up there on the left. If I look hard I could probably find myself on there, too. That was our little lot in the bottom right-hand corner. Look, we've all got little medals on. And as I recall all of the girls wore mauve ribbons.' (LS.)

SECTION FIVE

Events

PETER COOMBS, who later edited *the Journal of a Somerset Rector,* appears here as the ace of spades in 1923 on the Rectory lawn in Radstock.

ALMOST HIDDEN IN THE FLORAL DECORATION is two-year-old Doris Bird King who had just won a first prize in the garden fête at Norton House on 1 July, 1898.

LESLIE POLLARD pushes his sister Catherine in her carriage during the same fête in 1898. Leslie went on to become a Brigadier in the Royal Signals. Catherine is now living in Weston-super-Mare.

ALF AND BESSIE CARPENTER'S WEDDING PARTY in Radstock. Four of the Carpenter brothers served in the First World War and one of them, Arthur, was killed. Chris (Killup) Carpenter won the DCM as a sergeant with the Coldstream Guards.

A WEDDING IN MIDSOMER NORTON in the 1890s. I don't know who the couple is (I was given the picture as an unexposed negative) but I like the look of the party and this is my opportunity to show them off!

JUBILEE CELEBRATIONS (or the decorations, anyway) for the residents of Redfield Road in 1887.

FLOODWATER IN THE 1890s, pouring down through what used to be called The Island and into (what was then) The Market Place. The two portly characters on the left are standing directly above the original course of the river which was later diverted to its present route, behind the buildings to their rear.

PART OF THE HUGE CROWD THAT TURNED OUT IN MIDSOMER NORTON for the Proclamation of the Coronation of Edward VII in 1902.

A SOMEWHAT SMALLER TURNOUT but the town is still decked with bunting in 1910 when George V acceded to the throne.

THE GRAND OLYMPIAN CIRCUS visited Radstock in the 1920s, the horses being both performers and pullers of caravans.

MIDSOMER NORTON MARE AND FOAL SALE in 1911 with the auctioneers Blinman and Miles taking the bids. At this time horses and cattle were still sold in the streets during the annual carnival in November.

I'M TOLD THAT THIS IS NOT A CARNIVAL but a turnout of the Welton Jazz Band in around 1920. If it is, then I suspect that the unhappy clown closest to the camera is their chief comedian, Sam Cattell. The group was really a concert party which raised a great deal of money for charity.

CERTAINLY A MAJOR EVENT FOR MIDSOMER NORTON (and the most modern picture that I have ever printed). The unceremonious removal of the Jubilee Lamp in the 1950s.

SECTION SIX

Commerce

ELLEN BLAKE, who was born in 1885, used to help her father with his cooked meat shop and restaurant on Radstock Road before she left school. By the beginning of the Great War she had four children of her own and had opened a shop to sell light refreshments at the bottom of Redfield Road.

GILBERT PRIOR AND HIS SON GEORGE in his truck in which he delivered his mineral waters in 1916. 'And they were damn good but my cousin Albert always insisted on Brooks's stone ginger – from Bath. Mr Prior got to hear and got mad about it.' (CL.)

'THAT'S MR DENNING, the baker from Clandown, in Matticks' Yard behind the Waldegrave. Good bread t'was, too.' (CL.)

WELCH'S SHOP in Midsomer Norton was always known not only for its ambitious advertising but also for the quality of its goods. The pedestrians are blurred, probably because of the long camera exposure needed in 1897 rather than their hurry to get into the shop.

THE THREE HORSESHOES PUB in Midsomer Norton was demolished in recent years to make way for a supermarket.

'THAT'S ALB MITCHARD in the doorway, wearing a waistcoat – me uncle, and Aunt Minnie is over on the left. Bert is in the shirt and Ken, what kept the Railway Inn, is in the apron. T'other one is Fred. That's up the top of Welton Hollow in 1926.' (CL.)

A QUIET SCENE early this century with Sammy Lloyd's bakery on the left. Other shops in the row were Mr Prior's barber shop, Mr Angell's shoe shop and Mr Stenner's tobacconist shop.

ONE CART AND A CYCLE are the only vehicles to be seen on the Fosseway as it runs towards Radstock. The two young ladies on the left are at the door of Mr Mead's bakery.

'THIS IS MA RIVERS'S SHOP on Bath Hill, isn't it? The first photo I've seen of that. Well, well, well. We used to pop in there and spend our ha'pennies, farthings even – a stick of liquorice or something. Bullseyes, dolly mixture, nougat, sugary things – and things on sticks. Always cleared away for Sundays.' (GB) c.1905.

THE FRY FAMILY'S BLACKSMITHY on the left and the Midsomer Norton Post Office in the 1920s. 'My mother was the first postmistress there – I knew all the postmen. Oh, I like that coach-built pram. Six guineas we paid for one of those – a lot of money.' (LS.)

SECTION SEVEN

People

MEMBERS OF THE COMMITTEE responsible for organising Radstock's coronation festivities in 1902. Their programme included a number of services, social events and sporting activities, prizes for the latter consisting 'of an Assorted Collection of Various Useful and Ornamental Articles'.

DR WAUGH'S FAMILY in Midsomer Norton in 1890. Arthur Waugh, in the boater, later wrote *One Man's Road* which included some early reminiscences of the area. He was the father of Evelyn Waugh.

ANOTHER LOCAL FAMILY from the same period. 'I recognize 'em but I can't put a name to 'em 'cause they were much younger then. I had an outfit like the boys' – Norfolk jacket and nickey bockeys.' (CL.)

THIS IS ONE OF A NUMBER OF PICTURES found as undeveloped glass negatives following a fire in Midsomer Norton. Although we don't know who the young men were, the photographs are clearly a valuable source of information about life here at the turn of the century.

CROWDS IN RADSTOCK ON MARKET DAY in around 1910.

THE SHELLARD FAMILY OF GREENTREE FARM in Welton in 1911. It is interesting that they should have chosen to be photographed with the produce of their garden which was so extensive and well kept that it regularly attracted visitors out for their evening strolls.

MOSES HORLER, of Radstock, in 1900. 'I was born on the 7th day of July, in the year 1818. We were eight in the family and my eldest sister, Ruth, was born in the year 1799. We were all, with the exception of Ruth, born in the end cottage on Round Hill, built by my father 100 years ago (a portion of which appears in the illustration) . . .'.

A MIDSOMER NORTON TRADESMEN'S OUTING to Longleat before the First World War. Among those who went were Sammy Lloyd, the baker (with white trousers); butcher Honeybourne with his family and shoe shop owner Gregory with his. (The postcard was sent to me from South Africa by Mrs Gregory – née Honeybourne.) The party travelled in horse-drawn brakes hired from Matticks' Stables in Radstock. Sid Latchem, one of the drivers, is second from the left.

DR ALEXANDER WAUGH in around 1885. 'It was a life of hard, unremitting toil and sport was its only recompense. At any hour of the night there might come a knock on the door; and the sight of a horseman galloping up the lane put a premature end to many a gay day's shooting. But for the sportsman there was a relish even in uncertainty, and my father was a sportsman to the core.' (AW.)

YOUNG GEORGE TAYLOR (in the middle) with his family in around 1904 (notice how the photographer has added an absent sister to the picture). George won the Military Medal with the 6th Somersets in the First World War.

RADSTOCK'S TOWN CRIER, Joe Cottle, between the wars. Joe served with the Coldstream Guards during the first one.

'THAT'S WILLIAM TOVEY AND HIS FAMILY – used to live in the High Street. He was the man who built the houses at Hope Terrace and put his initials on the roofs of the first six. W.T.O.V.E.Y. Magnificent advertising.' (LS.)

'YES, THAT'S ME, down at the station in 1928, but that weredn't my taxi. Must've belonged to someone who'd caught a train. Made a picture though, di'nnit!' (CL.)

'JACK HILLIAR'S FIRST JOB was at Welton Brewery with Allan Thatcher. He went there when he was twelve and was there when war broke out. Then he went into the Machine Gun Corps.' (EH.)

'MY FATHER WAS A MEMBER OF THE ANCIENT ORDER OF FORESTERS and I joined as a juvenile and when we were 16 we were admitted into the adult group. Had our meetings where the Radstock Post Office is now.' (GB) c.1912.

A COUPLE OF UNIDENTIFIED YOUNG BLOODS from Midsomer Norton in the 1890s.

THE SIX LABOUR CANDIDATES for the Midsomer Norton Ward in the Urban District Council elections of 1935. The young man seated on the right later, as Sir Ronald Gould, became President of the World Confederation of Teachers' Organisations.

✦ Somerset County Council. ✦

~~~~~~~

JOSEPH BIRD thanks you for your support during the past six years, and solicits the favor of your **VOTE and INTEREST** at the Election, on

✦ **THURSDAY NEXT.** ✦

POLL EARLY at the

NATIONAL SCHOOLS, RADSTOCK.
NATIONAL SCHOOLS, PAULTON.
THE SCHOOLS, CAMERTON.

RADSTOCK'S COUNTY COUNCILLOR at the end of the last century issues his election message to his constituents. He was still their representative in 1902.

EMMA TUDGAY, of Radstock, licensed to sell tobacco. I am unsure if this Mrs Tudgay was related to the lady of the same name who was well known at Radstock Market.

GILBERT PRIOR – the mineral water manufacturer – takes young George for an outing.

Transport

'OUTSIDE MY UNCLE'S GARAGE in 1925 – somewhere about there, anyway. That's my brother Frank on the left, cousin Len, me and then Alf King, a teacher from Durham. That was the first petrol pump in the town!' (LS.)

WILLIAM H. HIGGINS – landlord of the Commercial Hotel – poses proudly with his pony and trap in 1911.

MR HIGGINS AGAIN, this time sitting in his brand new 1913, four seater 12/15 Mons motor car. Three months later, while driving through Terry Hill, outside Radstock, he stopped to light his acetylene lamps with a match and the whole car burst into flames so bright that they could be seen four miles away. The next day the Mattick brothers towed the wreck of a car (bought for £450) to Shearns Garage in Midsomer Norton.

A HORSE AND CART coming up Church Hill into Writhlington. 'Those swing boats are in Andrew Chivers's garden. We used to go along there on Chapel outings and sit on the bank to eat our buns.' (CL.)

THIS CARD WAS SENT TO MR AND MRS PIERCE of Midsomer Norton in 1907 by a family called Tucker from Radstock. The picture was taken by a man from Foxcote – so I believe that it is a local scene, but I can't work out where!

THE MIDSOMER-NORTON WAUGHS AT PLAY in 1883.

SECTION NINE
The Railways

A SUPERB SHOT of a Somerset and Dorset heavy goods locomotive positioned alongside Waterloo Road in Radstock.

'ABOUT THE TIME WHEN THIS WAS TAKEN (1904?) I went to work on the railways in Bristol but Father was Station Master here at Norton Hill and I'd been able to work the place since I was ten.' (DC.)

'WE CAME HERE IN 1890 and the signalman – a chap called Powell – taught me how to do all the signalling. Train in section, four knocks of the bell and so on. Could do the telegraph as well!' (DC.)

DRIVER EMERY, from Writhlington, filling the tank of his Radstock 'Dazzler' at Somerset and Dorset's locomotive shed in 1929.

A QUIET TIME ON THE BRISTOL LINE. The GWR station at Welton – 'Midsomer Norton and Welton' – in the first years of the century.

RADSTOCK NORTH GOODS YARD in the 1930s. 'Radstock in its hey-day! Used to unload cattle over there on the right. Its all pulled down down – houses built there. A different sort of Radstock.' (CL.)

A YOUNG LADY VISITOR surveys the scene on the Writhlington Collieries tramway in the early 1920s. The locomotive is a Peckett saddle-tank.

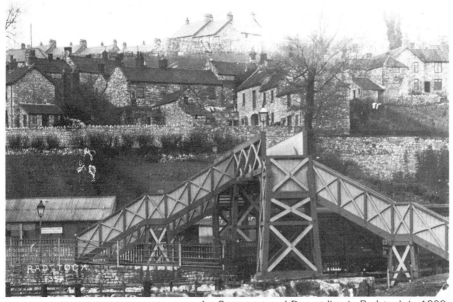

A RARE PICTURE OF THE FOOTBRIDGE over the Somerset and Dorset line in Radstock in 1909.

A BRISTOL-BOUND TRAIN comes to a halt at the up platform at the Great Western Railway station in Radstock in 1906.

ANOTHER VIEW OF THE GWR STATION in Radstock, taken between 1909 and 1915.

THE STAFF OF RADSTOCK NORTH STATION in 1907. The station-master was a Mr Latchem and his son, in the cloth cap on the left, was one of the office clerks.

ON 13 SEPTEMBER, 1902, 50 trains passed through the Somerset and Dorset station in a 12-hour period from 9a.m. It was a normal Saturday in Radstock.

SECTION TEN

Employment

THE REFURBISHING OF THE PALLADIUM in 1934. 'Stanley Foster did that. I saw the first cinematograph production in there when it was still the old Drill Hall. They had a stand in the middle and a man turned a handle and the flickers began. We were thrilled to bits there, in the dark.' (LS.)

WORKERS AT THE NORTH SOMERSET BRICK AND TILE COMPANY in Welton in the 1930s. From left to right, beginning at the back, they are: Boner Hamilton, Jim Snook, Jim Johnson, Isaac Prangley, Jim Dando, Reg Whittock, Stan Whittock, Arthur Johnson and Reg Howell, (no relation).

A POSTMAN pauses during his round of Westfield in 1908.

THE STAFF OF DR AND MRS BULLEID outside the Dymboro in Midsomer Norton. Mrs Bulleid's father was a successful sheep farmer in Australia and the house – built in 1908 – is said to have been his wedding present to her.

'WELL, I'M BLOWED. I worked there. Edwards' boot factory, up North Way in Midsomer Norton. Oh ah, I worked there. Matt Maggs were my foreman. Ollie Edwards were the boss.' (RJ.)

'OH-HO, THE HAYMAKING FIELD opposite Welton school on Radstock Road. That's Reuben Jones at the top of the ladder and Mr Mudford is the ladder man passing the stuff up. That's me in the big hat by Mr Whittock in the wheelchair!' (TB) c.1910.

SCYTHING IN UNDERHILL LANE, Midsomer Norton, at the turn of the century. 'Oh, that were enjoyable – see a rabbit scuttle out, and pheasants and partridges. Ah! Wonderful what you can see run out of the grass when you'm scythin'.' (IC.)

BUILDING WORKERS posing by the St Chad's Memorial in the 1890s. I am fascinated by the building in the background. Could it have been a temporary store room and shelter? If so it's a huge one.

ANOTHER PICTURE OF THE WORKMEN AT ST CHAD'S with one of them, curiously, holding a camera. The photograph was taken from a stereoscopic print, so maybe the camera belongs to the ambitious photographer.

MR WINES AND HIS WORKMEN at his yard in Radstock Road in the early 1930s. 'Very few could make a cart like that from start to finish – but Mr Wines could.' (LS.)

'CAW, THASS TOOK BACK A BIT! Thass the Writhlington Pigeon Fanciers, took outside Gill's ironmongery up opposite the Fir Tree. Round 1906 I reckon.' (CL.)

'THE OLD CO-OP STABLES along Waterloo Road. Behind there they used to slaughter cattle and things and we'd get an old pig's bladder — half full sometimes — and clean'n out and use for a football. Harry Dowling were responsible fer the horses here.' (CL) 1920.

A GANG OF BUILDERS on an unidentified site in Radstock. The picture was taken in 1912.

EMPLOYEES OF THE MIDSOMER NORTON URBAN DISTRICT COUNCIL outside the Council offices at the Town Hall in 1912.

SECTION ELEVEN

People

A WREATH LAYING CEREMONY in Midsomer Norton, soon after the Great War. This was before the War Memorial was moved to its present site over the river. Notice the poster on the right – 'Oh! A Dance – 6*d*.'.

'JOE RUDDOCK (back left) and his mates. There's George Dallimore, and Curry and Beard – and I know that chap's name by sight – there's Chivers, lived up Butter Buildings. That's round 1922ish. They've bin to a football match.' (CL.)

LOUIS BEAUCHAMP (back left), President of the Radstock amateur boxing club, with members at their first meeting in the scouts' hall in 1935. The boxer on the left in the vest is Fred Mitchard.

PIGEON FANCIERS in Midsomer Norton pose for their picture to be taken following a successful season soon after the First World War.

'PIGEON FANCIERS in Writhlington. That's a Foster and that's an Ashman, a Ponting, a Walters and that's a Riddick and that's my uncle, Walter Howell – but nothing to do with you!' (GB.)

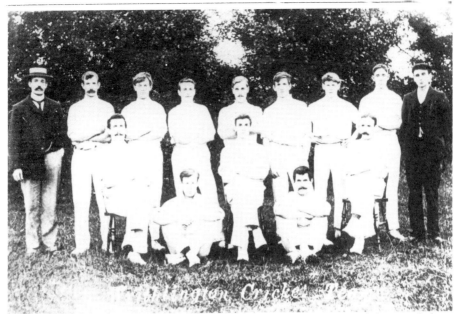

'GOSH, THESE WERE ALL WRITHLINGTON MEN — nearly all miners but one of these ended up Bishop of Malmsbury at the finish — Ronald Ramsey. Then I can see Alec Swift and Oliver Swift, and Hubert Ford and Seward Ford. Must be about 1906 or 7.' (GB.)

'NOW, THAT'S THE BOOZY BUFFS — the Ancient Order of Buffaloes in Radstock about 1920. Used to meet at the Waldegrave. Worthy Gait, Revd Aust, Sid Latchem, Gait, Gullick, Sage, Ford, Axford and that chap who used to play the piano and live up Westfield.' (CL.)

'I LIKE THIS ONE. Tom Brimble's Tyning Inn in 1924. Brimble had the smithy in Radstock at the same time. There's Joe Ruddock again, in the glasses – and Worthy Axford, Gait, Edwards and Charlie Gullick – and that's Joe's brother in the middle – the goalie – he were a policeman.' (CL.)

'MY COUSIN IVY MITCHARD (on the right) being given a bouquet at the Victoria Hall. She was one of the winners in the Radstock carnival queen competition in 1927.' (CL.)

THE MIDSOMER NORTON TENNIS SET in the 1920s. Doris Haydon (née King) is third from the left in the front row.

A CHARABANC OUTING from Stones Cross in the 1920s. 'I'll bet that that's a party from the chapel off to Cheddar and Wells – every excursion like that was to Cheddar and Wells.' (CL.)

THIS ONE WASN'T! These were all Midsomer Norton businessmen on their outing to the New Forest in 1914. Sammy Lloyd, the banker, is the prosperous-looking gent by the driver's door and Mr White, the photographer, is to his left with his little box of tricks.

'THE CHOIRMASTER OF THIS LOT WAS CHARLIE GREGORY, our teacher for Standard 4. He did rule we with a rod of iron. Bang! – if you didn't behave yourself, and we had to sing like bloody canaries!' (CL.)

SKIPPER BRUCE'S SCOUT TROOP in the 1930s. Back left is Leslie Shearn and back right is Bert Paget, standing beside Harry Edwards. In the front, with a wristwatch, is Frank Shearn and next to Frank, on the right, is my dad.

THE 'WESTFIELD FOLLIES' who were well known for their concert appearances in the late '20s and early '30s.

MIDSOMER NORTON'S SALVATION ARMY BAND in 1911.

MIDSOMER NORTON TRADESMEN engaging in a little horseplay in an early donkey derby on the meadow by St Chad's Well c.1928.

SPORTS DAY AT THE MEADOW. Colonel Pollard, the local GP, is holding the finishing tape on the right c.1910.

Churches

MIDSOMER NORTON'S HIGH STREET METHODISTS pose beside their church in 1905.

ARTHUR WAUGH, in 1931, wrote that: 'In the days when he was in retreat Charles the Second stayed at Midsomer Norton, and on his restoration bestowed upon the church an octave of bells. His memory was still honoured in the village on the 29th of May, when a club paraded the streets, with bands and banners, decked with oak leaves and oak apples'.

THE LADIES OF ST JOHN'S CHURCH, Midsomer Norton, in the 1920s. The three 'Waugh sisters' were all strong supporters of this church. 'They were identified with manifold village activities, classes for men and girls, tennis clubs, choral societies, amateur theatricals and nobody would have thought of suggesting that anyone of them should take up a profession.' (AW.)

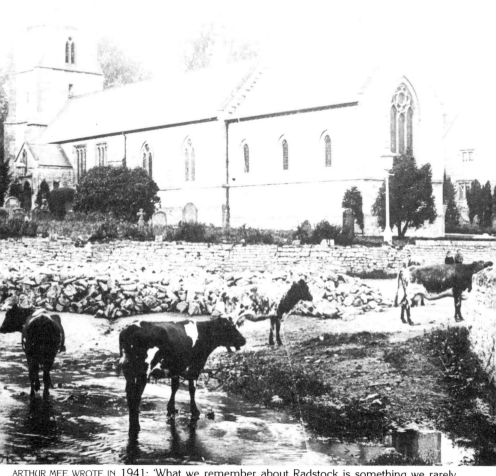

ARTHUR MEE WROTE IN 1941: 'What we remember about Radstock is something we rarely remember of any church, the Rectors List. It was done at the rectory when Canon Bax was there with his artist daughter, and we can almost see them enjoying the work of making up this bit of village history. We have seen no other Rectors List like it, and we found it more interesting than a hundred of last year's novels'.

THE CHURCH CHOIR AT RADSTOCK in 1885. Canon Coombs is on the right.

STONES CROSS CHAPEL CONGREGATION congregate outside. 'That was when religion was flourishing – now they're closing them down.' (LS.)

THE INTERIOR OF ST LUKE'S CHURCH, on Radstock Road. Sometimes known as the Metal Mission, the church has now been replaced by the Scout Hall.

A VIEW OF ST JOHN'S CHURCH in 1897.

THIS METHODIST GATHERING in the grounds of The Hollies provides a microcosm of life in Midsomer Norton in 1900. The newly-formed Male Voice Choir can be seen on the left – 'and there's Gareth Tovey; Richard Batt; Percy Tovey; one of the Gays – lovely voice; there's Fred Gould; and George Delve; and Robert Bennett; Melior; and that's one of the Thatchers from Stones Cross – always walked with his head down. I asked my father why and he said that Mr Thatcher had once picked up a sovereign and always after that . . .'. (LS.)

SECTION THIRTEEN

Schooling

WILLY GRANT, SCHOOLMASTER, with children from the National School in Midsomer Norton (now St John's) in 1905. 'It's silly but we used to think that we who went to the church school were a bit better than Wesleyans, mind. Church Rats and Chapel Mice. It's awful isn't it. But that used to give us pleasure!' (FC.)

AT ONE TIME, exercise for the children of the Wesleyan school in the High Street consisted of a walk around the river and back. Perhaps that's what they are doing here! *Circa* 1904.

GEORGE (DUCKY) DELVE, Headmaster of the Wesleyan school in Midsomer Norton, with his staff in 1912.

'NOW, THASS THE GARDENIN' SOCIETY run by old Mr Boulter. Well, I'm blowed. He used to train 'em. They used to have plots out in the Dymboro, behind St John's school – an' thass where thass took. Cuh! Thass old. Some o' they idn't more than 11–12 year old. Each man got his spade. Thass gotta be round nineteen five or six.' (RJ.)

RADSTOCK CHURCH OF ENGLAND SCHOOL in June 1912. The school was built in 1850 and, when this picture was taken, had about 400 pupils. These boys of the upper school are all sporting buttonholes for the occasion.

THE CHURCH SCHOOL in Midsomer Norton in 1923. The Headmaster, Mr Isaac Berrow Holmyard is seen here with Class I.

CHILDREN FROM THE HIGH STREET SCHOOL on their way to West Clewes, where Welton Rovers play, for their sports day in the 1930s. Notice the man in the church gates. So much tarmac has been laid in the town that the pillars are now barely four feet high.

THE SPORTS DAY MEETING. 'I was a sergeant in the specials during the last war and I went to that field to watch an exhibition by Joe Louis for the American troops. He moved like a cat – light as a feather. Anyone whoever'd been a policeman dug out his uniform to get in there. Old PC Drake had a hat on just like a pimple!' (LS.)

NORTON HOUSE in the 1920s when it was in use as St Michael's School, and its grounds as playing fields. Here the young ladies engage in a game of croquet.

CHILDREN FROM WELTON SCHOOL dress up, possibly for a carnival towards the end of the Great War. (Abe Lincoln's beard appears to need some adjustment!)

SECTION FOURTEEN
Wartime

FIFTEEN-YEAR-OLD FRANCES CRAIG from Dulwich who lied about her age in 1916 and joined the Land Army as a 17-year-old. She came to Somerset, fell in love with the horses, and stayed to work at Paulton Hospital until 1923.

I CAN'T SWEAR THAT THIS IS IN RADSTOCK but one of these volunteers from Chewton Mendip insists that they did leave from there in August 1914. 'In the beginnin' the miners didn' 'ave tuh go but when it come to the last goin' off – when they were gettin' short of men – they did draw names out of a hat of they miners what were illegible – down the Victoria Hall.' (JR.)

MEMBERS OF A TRANSPORT COMPANY of the Army Service Corps leaving Midsomer Norton towards the end of 1914.

THE BRISTOL ARTILLERY leaving Radstock following a recruiting visit.

SID LATCHEM, Radstock taxi proprietor, becomes Driver Latchem complete with his Crossley ambulance at Woolwich Barracks *en route* to Malta.

COLONEL POLLARD, Midsomer Norton doctor and officer commanding the territorial 4th Battalion Somerset Light Infantry, with his Midsomer Norton and Radstock warrant officers and sergeants.

COLONEL POLLARD and the whole of the 4th Battalion of the Somerset Light Infantry, in camp on Salisbury Plain, shortly before their departure for India. Much to his dismay and annoyance the Colonel was too old to accompany his men.

SOME OF THE PARTICIPANTS IN A CHARITY CARNIVAL that was arranged to collect money for Paulton Hospital during the War.

ONE OF THE FLOATS that were entered for the Paulton Hospital Carnival in 1915. Bo-peep and her attendants are seen waiting in the yard of the Welton Brewery, ready to take their place in the procession.

QUITE BY CHANCE I met these two people on the same day. They are two of the most considerate and courteous gentlemen I have ever met.

LESLIE POLLARD, the son of Colonel Pollard, was himself a subaltern in India in 1912.

SAMMY TAYLOR decided to leave the mines in 1912 and walked in to Bath to enlist in the Coldstream Guards. As a miner his boots had wedged between the roof and the floor of coal seams. As a soldier he was shot at Poperinghe. Sammy now lives in Chilcompton.

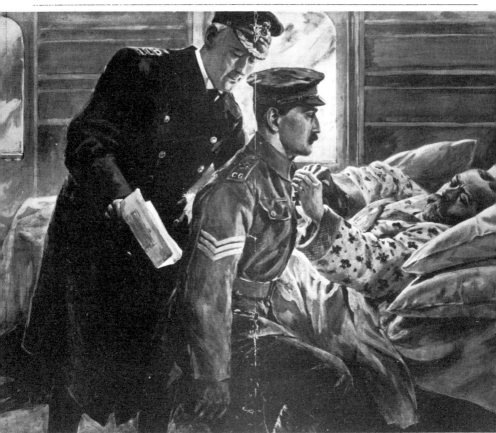

OLIVER BROOKS VC, of Midsomer Norton receiving his medal in a railway carriage, from King George who was suffering from the after-effects of a fall from his horse. Jack Brooks, as he was known to his friends, was a Coldstreamer who had fought off German soldiers pouring into the British trenches. On his triumphant homecoming, his train stopped as scheduled in Radstock, where his cousin Stuart Brooks spotted him. 'He had his hand underneath the medal showing it to Mr Simpkins from the pit. Then he saw me and wound the window down and asked where his dad was. I told him that everyone was at Norton Hill waiting for him. "I'm glad I met you", he said and the train started moving off.' The reception Oliver received in Midsomer Norton was tumultuous.

COLONEL POLLARD, Medical officer in charge, seated with the ladies of the local VAD (Somerset 28) outside Midsomer Norton Secondary School which, in 1915, was in use as a military hospital. His daughter Catherine – with the glasses – is seated between him and Miss Constance Waugh. Eustace Welch is the gentleman at the back.

THE CEREMONIAL UNVEILING OF THE WAR MEMORIAL in Radstock in 1919.

FORMER AND EXISTING SERVICEMEN form up together on the left during the dedication of Midsomer Norton's War Memorial in 1919.

'DURING THE SECOND WORLD WAR, the American Fifth Army had its headquarters where Faulkners, the Solicitors are now, in Midsomer Norton. Their various units were dispersed all around the area. And they had a huge band, all padding along on soft shoes.' (LS.)

SECTION FIFTEEN

Charlie Fry

ALAN CHIVERS AND JOHNNIE WINDLESS WITH BOXER AND CHARLIE FRY. Alan: 'He wasn't my boss and I wasn't his labourer. We were mates. The 50 years between us was nothing to me. He sounded so rough that people who didn't know him couldn't understand how a little kid like me could be with Charlie. But he had such a way with him. I loved him. And I went on loving him as I grew up, though I never really thought of it as that until now.'

151

CHARLIE LIVED WITH HIS FAMILY in Clapton until he was 23. As well as the smithy in Midsomer Norton and the farm at Coomber's Grave, the Frys also had a smallholding behind their home. Charlie's mother 'was a cheddar cheese maker and butter maker. And we kept pigs – fat pigs – and wean calves. We did have veal for our Sunday dinners, our own home-cured veal.' (CF.)

CHARLIE PRATTEN'S CLASS at the Wesleyan School in Rackvernal Road, before it moved to the High Street site. All of the Fry children attended this school, travelling down in Mr James's covered wagon until they were eight-years-old, after which they had to walk. Mr Delve was the Head then and both he and his wife were good to the Frys. 'If ever we turned up from Clapton with wet clothes Mrs Delve'd always take them from us and dry them.' (CF.)

THE FRYS' BLACKSMITH SHOP in Midsomer Norton. 'Charlie's sister Flo worked in there. She were a striker when we made the bonds for Taylor's big timber wagons. When they were heated and out on the anvil Lemuel would be turnin' of 'em with the grips and I and Flo had seven pound sledges. I were on one side an' she on t'other. Bang. Bang. Bang. Bang. She were as hard as any man.' (IC.)

'HE TOLD ME THAT WHEN YOU MAKE A RICK you always had to make sure that there was no plantain in it, 'cause that could cause a rick fire. Lots I learnt like that. I don't know what I did for him. I did cut his hair, though. I'd take some scissors from home and he'd sit under a tree and I'd snip, snip, snip at it. No style – anything but. Me a 10, 11, 12-year-old.' (AC.)

'WHEN HE DID GO TO THE FAIR HE DID DRESS UP PROPER. Brown boots, brown leather leggin's, fawn britches and a sports coat and very likely – more often than not – he'd have a walking stick. He were always known for his smartness in the olden days.' (IC.)

'HE WAS ALWAYS POLITE. I can see him saying "Hello" to my sister now and he'd always call her Miss – just like he did his own sister. I never heard him call anyone by their first name – certainly not his own family.' (AC.)

CHARLIE FRY joined the Coldstream Guards on 10 December 1915. He was at Passchendaele. He came home with trench feet (which were so rotten the bones of his leg were visible) and with a disturbed mind.

'MISS FRY used to always prepare his food. I never saw him eat off a plate, always in a basin. Bread and scrape. Clean out his basin with a doorstep of bread and guzzle cold, milky tea from a lemonade bottle with tea leaves swirling and jumping about.' (AC.)

'HIS WAY OF LIFE was such that as long as he was busy, with a meal and a roof over his head, that was all he would worry about. He'd milk a few cows or go to the pit for some bag coal for pensioners, he was happy. Money was of no interest to him whatsoever. Never important. I learnt so much from him. He's the sort of person no-one could ever forget. You sort of carry him with you.' (AC.) Charlie Fry had a heart attack while driving his cart in 1955. Before he died he asked the doctor to see to it that his pony was going to be all right.

ACKNOWLEDGEMENTS

These books are always a compilation of other people's words and pictures and all of those whose names follow have contributed in some way, be it great or not quite so great. One or two made contributions that were fundamental to the actual appearance of the book, Dick Graham was one (the cover picture is his). Although I have only quoted Alan Chivers a few times I am particularly grateful to him. I have at last printed a few of the words he gave me when we talked about Charlie Fry – we talked for several hours and I cried again when I typed some of them. Then I thank that little gang of pals I turn to when I'm stuck for a picture or an idea – they know who they are and their names appear in the following list.

Those pictures that were not my own came from: Peter Bates (St Nicholas School, Radstock), Tom Bull, Mrs J. Clarke, Peter Coombs, Frances Craig, M. Denning, Bert Elford, Gordon and Mary Fry, Mrs J. Garrett, Dick Graham, Chris Handley, Elsie Hilliar, Cliff Latchem, Gwen Malcolm, Fred Mitchard, Bob Parsons, David Patch, Catherine Pollard, Mrs Posselwhite, Bob Powell, Mrs G. Prior, Tom Randall, Dennis Rendall, Gwen Ricketts, Leslie Shearn, Richard Shearn, Lena Siek, Jack Simmonds, George Taylor, Sammy Taylor, Miss Tovey, Norman Voake, Mr Vranch and Terry Whittock.

The words, other than my own, are those of Tom Bull, George Brown, Ellen Blake, Stuart Brooks, Dennis Caines, Flo Chivers, Bill Curtis, Ivan Chard, Constance Fry, Jack Gait, Elsie Hilliar, Reg Jones, Cliff Latchem, Joe Ruddock, Leslie Shearn and Sammy Taylor, but not – for the first time – Austin Wookey!